# EIGHT YEARS AND A DAY

## *Dale Stivers*
### a.k.a Benjamin Christian

**TEACH Services, Inc.**
PUBLISHING
www.TEACHServices.com • (800) 367-1844

World rights reserved. This book or any portion thereof may not be copied or reproduced in any form or manner whatever, except as provided by law, without the written permission of the publisher, except by a reviewer who may quote brief passages in a review.

The author assumes full responsibility for the accuracy of all facts and quotations as cited in this book. The opinions expressed in this book are the author's personal views and interpretations, and do not necessarily reflect those of the publisher.

This book is provided with the understanding that the publisher is not engaged in giving spiritual, legal, medical, or other professional advice. If authoritative advice is needed, the reader should seek the counsel of a competent professional.

Copyright © 2023 Dale Stivers
Copyright © 2023 TEACH Services, Inc.
ISBN-13: 978-1-4796-1489-9 (Paperback)
ISBN-13: 978-1-4796-1490-5 (ePub)
Library of Congress Control Number: 2022920154

All scripture quotations, unless otherwise indicated, are taken from the King James Version (KJV). Public Domain.

Scripture quotations marked ESV are taken from The Holy Bible, English Standard Version. ESV® Text Edition: 2016. Copyright © 2001 by Crossway Bibles, a publishing ministry of Good News Publishers.

Scripture quotations marked NKJV are taken from the New King James Version®. Copyright © 1982 by Thomas Nelson. Used by permission. All rights reserved.

Scripture quotations marked NIV are taken from THE HOLY BIBLE, NEW INTERNATIONAL VERSION®, NIV® Copyright © 1973, 1978, 1984, 2011 by Biblica, Inc.® Used by permission. All rights reserved worldwide.

Published by

www.TEACHServices.com • (800) 367-1844

# Table of Contents

*Foreword* . . . . . . . . . . . . . . . . . . . . . . . . . . . . . . . . . . . *iv*
*Special Thanks To—* . . . . . . . . . . . . . . . . . . . . . . . . . . . *v*
*Before You Read This Book* . . . . . . . . . . . . . . . . . . . . . . *vi*

1. Punished by the Law . . . . . . . . . . . . . . . . . . . . . . . 7
2. Why I Was Arrested—An Attempted Rape that Went Wrong! . . . . . . . .13
3. Love Stinks. . . . . . . . . . . . . . . . . . . . . . . . . . . . .17
4. How I Got Started into Pornography . . . . . . . . . . . . . . .22
5. The Power of Porn. . . . . . . . . . . . . . . . . . . . . . . . .26
6. The Beauty and the Beast. . . . . . . . . . . . . . . . . . . . .30
7. Why Men Like to Watch Sex . . . . . . . . . . . . . . . . . . . .34
8. An Introduction to God. . . . . . . . . . . . . . . . . . . . . .37
9. Understanding the Bible . . . . . . . . . . . . . . . . . . . . .40
10. God's Son Can Help You! . . . . . . . . . . . . . . . . . . . . .45
11. Asking for Forgiveness . . . . . . . . . . . . . . . . . . . . . .48
12. God or the Twelve-Step Program? . . . . . . . . . . . . . . . .51

*Why I Wrote This Kind of a Book?* . . . . . . . . . . . . . . . . . .55
*A Day* . . . . . . . . . . . . . . . . . . . . . . . . . . . . . . . . . . . . .58
*Appendix* . . . . . . . . . . . . . . . . . . . . . . . . . . . . . . . . . .60

# Foreword

## By Pastor Joe Gresham of the Seventh-day Adventist Church

I have known the author of this book for several years and know that he is a dedicated Christian with a longing desire to share his love for God and His forgiveness of actions that had brought shame, pain, and reproach upon himself, his God, and many others. It is his desire to share with others, through this book, that the power and love of God that he found are available to all who will believe and accept the unconditional, all-pervading love and forgiveness that God has for all who will turn to Him in repentance, and, realizing that through the blood of Jesus, he or she will be able to stand before God as if they had never sinned. Praise God, and may this work prove to be a blessing to you and accomplish the purpose for which it was written.

Joe W. Gresham

# Special Thanks To—

I want to pay special thanks to Mark Anthony (a former Las Vegas casino owner and famous chef) who encouraged me and suggested the official title for this book, "Eight Years and a Day" from my original title, "Eight Years—My Side of the Story." And to Donna L. Ferrier who patiently and professionally edited my manuscript to make it possible for readers to understand the message of this book. I owe her a noticeably BIG thank you! And to Pastor Joe Gresham for taking the time out to read through this material and write a thoughtful foreword to this book.

# Before You Read This Book

This is my real story of how I fell into pornography through rejection from girls and women. I have used pseudonyms to protect the individuals' identity!

When I first wrote this book, I was writing to a targeted audience. But my publishing editors told me that they couldn't edit the manuscript because it contained a lot of graphic material. Pastor Joe Gresham pointed out to me that I wouldn't know how to reach the targeted audience, and the general reading public wouldn't accept the graphic material that was in there and would turn them off from reading it. So, I went back in and changed and re-edited almost half of the book to make it more available to the general public instead of a targeted audience. Warning: this is a true account of my life that I am sharing with you. I had a terrible addiction that I kept secret from my family and most of the general public where I grew up. Only a few of my friends knew that I had this addiction! And now, I am sharing it with you, hoping that my story might help someone else who has the same addiction that I had. My addiction was to pornography! I was a super, very hard-core pornographer for more than twenty-eight years!

CHAPTER 1

# Punished by the Law

It was early Friday morning, March 15, 2002, at about 12:45 a.m. I was sitting at my computer searching the web from my bedroom in Houston, Texas, when I heard a knock at the front door. *Who could that be at this time of night?* I wondered, afraid to answer it. The knock came again. Midnight, one of my cats, meowed as if she was asking me, *Who is at the front door?* I got out of my chair, walked to the front door, and yelled, "Who is it?"

Another loud voice answered back: "Harris County sheriff. Open up."

"Give me a minute to get dressed," I responded as I walked back to my bedroom to put on a pair of pants and a pullover shirt. When I came back out, I turned on the two floor lamps next to the front door. I knew why the sheriff had come; I just didn't think he'd come this soon. When I opened the door, I saw the detective and four other officers. He motioned for me to step outside as if he wanted a word with me. As soon as I stepped out, he told me to put my hands behind my back, after which he placed the cold, steel handcuffs around my wrists. Then one of the officers turned me around and shoved me back through my apartment door as the detective and the other officers entered behind me. The door closed, and all of us were standing in the living room. The detective read me my rights. "What am I being arrested for?" I asked.

"You're being charged with aggravated assault with a deadly weapon and aggravated kidnapping on Julie Anderson," he responded. Both my cats, Midnight and Socks, were meowing loudly as if they were asking, *Who are these people? What is going on?* I was still in my bare feet, so I asked if I could go to the bedroom and put on my tennis shoes before we left. One of the officers helped me get the shoes onto my feet. I wanted to get my watch off the dresser, but the officer informed me I wouldn't need it. He did allow me to take my wallet, however, and asked where the apartment key was. When I pointed it out on my keychain, he led me back into the living room again. The four deputy sheriffs rummaged through my kitchen drawers and cabinets, my dresser, closet, and my bathroom drawers like they had a search warrant, but I knew they wouldn't find anything. I did complain that the cuffs were too tight on my wrists and asked the deputies if they could loosen them a bit. One of the officers readjusted them, but it didn't help. The detective waved his hand for everyone to leave, and the deputies led me outside, making sure the cats didn't escape through the front door.

As the detective was locking the door, my neighbor across the hall came out of his apartment, shocked to see the deputies leading me away in handcuffs. "Oh, no, what's happening?" cried the neighbor. One of the officers told her it was none of her business, and they led me down three flights of stairs and outside. My taxi that I had started as my own business was parked out front by the stairs, and we passed it en route to the sheriff's car, where the deputies put me into the back seat. A big, husky guy like me, who weighs 300 pounds, is very difficult to load into a squad car. It's definitely not as easy as it looks on television, where the officers just tuck the person's head down and zip them inside. First, they tried to put me in, leading with one leg at a time. When that didn't work, they turned me around, sat me down sideways, and moved me backward along the back seat until I was able to get both feet inside.

As we pulled out of my apartment complex, I wondered whether I'd ever see my apartment or my two cats again. On the way to the jail, one of the officers was trying to recall the song "In the Jailhouse Now" from the movie *O Brother, Where Art Thou?* by the Soggy Bottom Boys. I think he was applying it to me. My wrists began to swell inside the cuffs, cutting off my circulation to my fingers.

We arrived at the sheriff's substation holding center at about 1:30 a.m. By this time, my hands were turning light blue, and I had no feeling in them when one of the officers took the cuffs off. He started laughing as he watched me try to get circulation back into my hands.

"Oh, it wasn't that bad," he mused.

I cursed at him for having the cuffs on too tight in the first place, which made him laugh even more. Eventually, he escorted me inside the station and instructed me to sign some paperwork. One of the female officers became angry when she saw that I was actually reading the papers before signing them, but I wanted to know what I was agreeing to.

When the police took the mug shot, I gave the dirtiest look ever (see Appendix). Then I had to wait about forty-five minutes for the paddy wagon to transport me, along with several other men and women, to the main jailhouse in Houston. I am not going to describe going through the process of being locked up in a city/county jail facility. It's bad enough being arrested, but going through all the procedures is even worse and humiliating. My world as I knew it was now coming apart! I was now living in a nightmare that was new to me because I'd never been in this situation before.

There was no bunk bed for me to sleep on because the jail pod, which holds twenty men, was overcrowded! My thin, two-inch mattress was on the floor with a pillow for me to sleep on. Sitting on the mattress gave me time to think over what had happened in my life to lead up to this arrest and sitting inside a jail pod along with the rest of the inmates who messed up their own lives as I had! Who to blame? I had to blame someone for getting me into this mess! For years and years, I blamed the girls I grew up with at school and my failed love life. See chapter three, Love Stinks. But looking back, I was wrong in thinking that. I was the one to blame! Being pudgy and fat growing up makes it hard to be liked and accepted around other people. Did I have an obnoxious character? No, I was totally the opposite! I do have a sensitive side to me, and I believe I was using food as a comfort zone.

> *All I wanted was for the other kids to accept me for who I was as I accepted them for who they were.*

I grew up without a father. My father died when I was only twelve years old. My mother never remarried. All I wanted was for the other kids to accept me for who I was as I accepted them for who they were. I had no problem accepting other kids as friends. But I couldn't understand why they didn't accept me. I had no father figure to guide me along growing up. All I wanted was to be liked, and I was not getting that. Then I started noticing girls. And that made it even worse! I wish that someone would have pointed out to me that girls don't think the same way as boys do! I was in a world of looks and attractiveness misunderstanding. My perception was that cute and attractive girls have sweet and pleasant personalities, and plain to ugly girls have mean and hateful personalities!

Being made fun of at school by the girls in my class, I turned to pornography out of curiosity, but mostly as an escape from the rejection of the girls I knew at school. It was the wrong path to follow. But it was offering me the acceptance from the rejection I was feeling at school. That led me into a nearly twenty-eight-year hard-core addiction! I felt that through pornography, I could beat the rejection and not feel rejected anymore! But all of that was A LIE! First, it was going to the adult book stores along East Colfax in Denver, Colorado.

Then, moving up to the adult movie theater to see XXX-rated films that had just come out. And other things that I won't mention. Pornography was filling the void; at least, I thought it was.

Then I met a certain girl, whom I tell you all about in chapter two. But being in that jail pod or that facility building was a wake-up call to me in my life that something had to change! This was all a new experience to me, and I didn't know what type of prison sentence I would get and how long I would be locked up in prison. I needed to study and learn the law because I broke it by harming my victim. I asked some other inmates what law books I needed to read to know to help me out of my case. They told me which ones to read and study, and I was able to get the information to get the DA to change my sentence from thirty-five years to fifteen years!

I was appointed a court attorney, to whom I told the truth about what happened that night with Julie and how I harmed her and accidentally slashed her right arm with my large bow knife that I had in my hand, trying to scare her into submission! I had three DA plea bargain deals with the court DA, and on the third try, he when down from fifteen years to eight years! That was on July 12, 2002. And on that date, I was sentenced to eight years inside a TDCJ (Texas Department County of Justice) prison. From March 15 to October 2002, I was in a jail facility, and I was moved to three different jail pods.

I was raised a Christian, but pornography took over and interfered with my relationship with God. In the first jail pod where I landed, I had two very deep religious encounters with Holy Spirit. One of them is told later on in this book. Over a few months, I knew that I needed to get reacquainted with the Lord again by reading the Bible. I started with the gospels, Matthew, Mark, Luke, and John. From there, I went to Romans,

Galatians, Ephesians, First and Second Timothy, and First and Second Peter. I met a Jehovah's Witness inmate, and we became friends, sharing each other's beliefs and faith. But God was using this jail and prison scenario to "dry me out" of my pornography addiction that I had indulged in for twenty-eight years.

To me, eight years in prison was a long time! I knew that I had to change. I knew that only a relationship with God could bring about this change. I wanted to witness to other inmates. But where would I go? What type of prison will they send me to? A friendly prison or a hard, rock n' roll prison where everyone fights every day? These were the types of thoughts going through my mind as I awaited my jail-to-prison transfer. *Welcome home, Dale,* I thought. *Looks like you're going to be here awhile.*

CHAPTER 2

# Why I Was Arrested—
# An Attempted Rape
# that Went Wrong!

Julie was a very stunning and attractive eighteen-year-old girl. She looked a lot like Mary-Kate Olsen from the TV sitcom show *Full House*. She'd contacted me through my county cab business to take her to work at Walmart and bring her home. She was a high school senior at Spring High School off I-45 who worked part-time on the weekends.

Soon, she became one of my regular customers, and unbeknownst to her, I was quite attracted to her. She also lived close to the apartment where I was living. I'd never been married before and was about to turn forty-four. I lived alone in a one-bedroom apartment with my two cats to keep me company. I was also overweight by a good 130 pounds, so my self-esteem was pretty low.

Just prior to February 23, 2002, I was working anywhere from eighty to a hundred hours a week, and I was desperately trying to lose weight. A famous late night/early morning talk show radio host on the AM dial I listened to every night advertised a weight-loss pill called "Ultra Slim™" About a month before February 23, I ordered the product and was popping pills like crazy. But the overdose produced a side effect similar to that produced by methamphetamines. So, if nothing else, it gave me a good high buzz to keep me awake during those long hours of work.

On the morning of February 23, I popped my overdose of Ultra Slim and was set to go. Julie called me around 9:00 a.m. and asked me to pick her up before 11:00 and return at 11:00 that night to take her home. But when I dropped her off that Saturday morning, something in my mind snapped, and I picked her up in a city taxi instead of my county taxi. Deep down, I'd been in love with this girl since the first day I took her to work. Being around her just made me want to open myself up like a book and tell her everything about my life—all my secrets, my philosophy, my dating life, and all my hopes, dreams, and plans for the future. Given the chance, I would have slipped a wedding ring on her finger and married her on the spot. She had an effect on me that I could not describe. It was not infatuation. More like obsession!

My love for Julie was driving me crazy! But I knew that our age difference was very lopsided. Here I was, a forty-three-year-old single man who was deeply in love with an eighteen-year-old girl!

Plus, I was a twenty-eight-year addict to porn to boot. It sounds like a pedophile situation to me, but a pedophile doesn't marry the person with whom he wants to have sex. So, in my porn mind, I developed a plan to "force her into submitting to me and my love for her." I was going to

1.) kidnap her, and 2.) I was going to rape her into submission no matter how long it took in the back seat of my taxicab. I don't know where my mind was! I cannot force a woman into loving me.

Please note: Yes, I did kidnap Julie by lying to her when I picked her up at Walmart when she got off work. I told her that I was going a different way back to her apartment complex. But I drove her to a very exclusive hide-out spot, where no one could see us at all or hear her screams and cries while I was doing my evil deed to her. It was deep in the woods and out of sight. My plan was very sexually sick in what I wanted to do to Julie in forcing my sick sexual love for her!

That was my line of thinking and reasoning, and boy, was I way off base! But when I tried to rape her, that's when everything went **WRONG.** Praise God! First of all, I didn't rape her! I never got to lay a hand on her. Second, she kicked the living daylights out of me from the back seat of the taxicab. And third, she accidentally got cut on her right arm by my big bowie knife that was at least ten to twelve inches in length. I was mainly using it to scare her into submission and to get her out of her clothes! But that never happened! No clothes came off, and I never touched her at all. She took me by surprise by putting up a good fight from the back seat. She also tried to gouge my eyes out with her fingers. I never got the chance to get in the back seat with her. But I do regret accidentally slashing her wrist or arm with my bowie knife! She is going to have that scar for the rest of her life.

When she screamed, "I'm bleeding!" my heart sank so low. I knew that I had to make a sudden choice: one, jump over from the driver's seat into the back seat with my victim, rip her clothes off, and rape her while she was bleeding, or two, call the whole thing off and drive her back home and drop her off. I chose the latter. While driving her home, I was tempted to go to the North Houston Hospital off of FM (farm to market road) 1960. But I was afraid that if I took her to the emergency room at the hospital that she would cry "rape" inside, and I would be arrested on the spot. So, I took her home to the apartment complex. She and I talked a little bit when I dropped her off, and then she ran back to her apartment.

I don't know whether she ever told her mom and dad, but she or her parents called 911, and the sheriff's department came to her home. They took a police report of the incident and called an ambulance to take her to the hospital, where she received medical treatment and some stitches for her right arm.

CHAPTER 3

# Love Stinks

In the 1980s, the J. Giles Band released a song that describes my relationships with other women perfectly, "Love Stinks." The first girl who ever showed any interest in me was a girl named Sally back in the first grade. During recess one day, Sally and I were sitting alone near a window ledge while the other kids were playing somewhere else. She leaned toward me as if she wanted to kiss me. Unfortunately, while I realized what she was doing, I was still too young to understand the importance of it. And having a "he-man" kind of mentality that boys don't kiss girls because girls gave them "cooties," I punched Sally in the nose. As she ran off with her bloody nose, crying to our teacher, I was proud that I defended myself against a girl who wanted to give me cooties.

It wasn't until third grade that my views changed, and I noticed a girl in our class named Crystal. I was attracted to her, but she wasn't attracted to me. Both her girlfriends and her older brother, who was two grades ahead of me, told me she wasn't interested in me at all. But somehow, I wasn't taking the hint and needed her to tell me herself. I mean, I was fat—not exactly the popular kid in school—so I figured that's why her friends didn't like me. But after chasing her for two years, I finally gave up and let her go. She obviously didn't want any close friendship with me, and that sting of rejection hurt.

By the sixth grade, my hormones started kicking in, and I began noticing more girls in our classroom and how good they looked. But I also realized none of them wanted anything to do with me. Girls in junior high labeled me as the number one loser, which did nothing to enhance my self-image. Without any friends to turn to, I gained more and more weight. During my freshman year of high school, two girls flirted with me just as a game to get my hopes up for a relationship, only to make fun of me and make me feel rejected by every girl in school.

> *Without any friends to turn to, I gained more and more weight.*

There was one I really liked while I was a freshman. The crush I had on her was similar to the one I had on Crystal. But I didn't want to let her know how I felt for fear I'd be let down by my own wishful thinking. In the end, however, she was nice when she let me down. She just felt the age difference was too great but thought it was sweet that I had a crush on her.

I chased after a girl who was a year ahead of me in my sophomore year. She wanted no part of me at all. Word got around that I had a super crush on her, which made her even more distant. So, by this time, I was a good sixty to eighty pounds overweight and had low self-esteem from all the rejection, which kept me from trying to lose the weight. I didn't view my weight as the problem, even though I couldn't identify what the problem was that always put me at odds with the opposite gender. I just thought I was jinxed and that no one would ever want me as a boyfriend. When I was in eighth grade, I came up with this scenario of a courtroom setting called "Act One," where I was inside of a legal courtroom, and I was on trial for liking girls. The verdict said that I was found "guilty" and was sentenced to never look at or like any girls again! I wrote it out in my frustration on my feeling towards females.. I became convinced in my mind that all females passed judgment on me, and now it was them against me!

When I started my senior year of high school, I transferred to a private Christian boarding academy far away from the school I'd been attending. It was there I met the girl of my dreams, the girl I wanted to marry and spend the rest of my life with. Her name was Bunny. We struck up a mutual friendship, but I loved her from afar. I never tried to date her because she was dating somebody else. There was another young girl, a freshman named Roberta. She was sweet but not as attractive as Bunny. If you've ever seen the sitcom "Ugly Betty," that's a fairly good description of Roberta, minus the braces and with shorter hair. Roberta was also shy and kept to herself. One of the popular teachers at the school repeatedly joked that Roberta was my girlfriend and that we'd get married someday. Even though the teasing was all in good fun, and the teacher meant no harm, both Roberta and I reacted negatively to it while the teacher walked away laughing. It put the idea in her head that I couldn't be "the one" for her. Near the end of the school year, Roberta started opening up to me, but I still had my eye on Bunny. But after graduation in 1977, Bunny and I went our separate ways. I returned to my mother and brother in Denver to live at home.

I tried my best to forget about Bunny, but being away from her made me want her all the more. She was constantly on my mind. My heart ached for her. I did some stupid stuff in trying to forget her, which led to more pain for myself because I feel her presence as if she was actually there witnessing it and crying in the background, my love for her had driven me to despair.

About the time Bunny got married, I got engaged to Roberta, but that didn't last either. I was still living in Colorado, and she was living in Pennsylvania. About a month into the engagement, I broke my right leg one Saturday night, while learning how to roller skate, which made traveling to Pennsylvania to bring her home as my wife more difficult. Of course, all of this was planned behind my mother's back because she didn't want any female to come between her and her last son to take care of her, so she was determined to keep me single until she died. After corresponding back and forth for about seven months, Roberta dropped me.

Years went by, and after I tried a few matchmaking rip-off companies, I'd had it with dating altogether. Sometime in the fall of 1984 or 1985, I placed an ad in the personals column in the *Rocky Mountain News*, a local newspaper in Denver. It was a general marriage proposal to unmarried females. It ran for one week and turned out to be one of the stupidest ideas that I had. I did, however, meet one incredibly attractive female who looked like a professional model but strung me along. On our first date, she said yes to my marriage proposal, but afterward, I discovered she'd been living with her boyfriend for five years in another state, and the two had just broken up. About five days later, the boyfriend showed up and proposed to her. She accepted his proposal and dumped me.

The last girl I got serious about was Carol. I met her on a "Christian" Internet dating service in the fall of 2000. We started leaving each other email messages. One night in the early part of January 2001, she called me on the phone to surprise me, and we talked for about two hours. From then on, we called each other every day. But I was living in Texas at that point, and she was living in Tennessee. The weekend after Valentine's Day, I flew to Chattanooga to meet her and her parents. Unfortunately, her parents quickly sized me up and decided they didn't like me. Both Carol and I hit it off, though, and we were determined not to let distance become a problem. Carol and I were true to our promise to each other, and we called each other every day.

In April, I drove from Houston to her parents' place just outside Chattanooga for the weekend. Unfortunately, as our love for each other grew stronger, so did her parents' hatred of me. In May, she drove to Houston for a weekend visit, and on Mother's Day 2001, I took her to a nice Italian restaurant. By this time, given the long-distance nature of our relationship, I wanted a firm commitment that she wouldn't see anyone else. So, during the meal, I got down on one knee, engagement ring in hand, and proposed. Carol took a long time to say, "Yes," but we agreed we would marry immediately after she graduated college.

Right after we got back to my apartment, we called her parents and told them the good news. They didn't take it well. "Oh really?" said the father in a very disgusted voice. From that night on, they did everything they could to convince her to dump me. In June, I warned Carol that her parents would try to break us up, but she wouldn't listen. By July, I could tell they were straining our relationship. One night in September 2001, as we were talking on the phone, she finally told me that her love for me was all dried up and that she was calling off the engagement, citing her parents' pressure. And since her love for her parents was stronger than her love for me, I wasn't going to fight with her, so we parted as friends. Sadly, she was still single for eight more years after we broke up.

Since the breakup, I've been on countless one-evening-type dates, I've been dropped numerous times, and I've been stood up on blind dates. I've felt the countless failures of never getting the "dream girl" and being cheated out of love. Oh, yeah, love stinks! You just read my lifelong failures with women. But were they all failures? No, they were not. Looking back on those relationships, I did things that were wrong that caused the end of the relationship or chased after some woman that I shouldn't have.

I used pornography as a focal point in trying to have a relationship with a woman. I needed to see a different way to have a relationship with a woman and learn to have a correct one. And not knowing what was the correct way of dating and how to attract a female properly to fall in love with, I was at fault! And because my mind was so filled up with pornography, that's what really **STINKS!**

CHAPTER 4

# How I Got Started into Pornography

A woman friend of my mother's, who went to nursing school with her, had a son named Tony, who had a lot of *Playboy* magazines in his basement bedroom. Tony was a year younger than my middle brother Douglas, and every time we would visit, he would bring out two or three magazines when my brother and I went to his room. But that did not get me hooked on pornography! I was a young boy of nine or ten and thought that seeing a beautiful naked woman was the most beautiful thing or sight in the world. I was not into sex at that age or understood what intercourse was about. My parents were not shy about talking to us kids about sex when we were growing up. But we also were told that it was a personal or family matter and not to talk about it to anyone else outside the family. I started liking girls at a young age. Not for sex or kissing or holding hands but to have as a playmate, a friend, and someone to be my close friend.

In the last chapter, I mentioned how girls treated me at school while growing up slightly overweight. I felt that no girl in the world was interested in me just as a friend and nothing more. I didn't know how to date, what girls were interested in, their mindset, their thinking, and what attracted them to boys. I was clueless because of non-acceptance and being a target of humiliation. Hello to adult XXX bookstores in 1974. The constant rejection, put-downs, and public humiliation at school drove me into the waiting open arms of pornography. I had just started as a freshman in high school, and I knew that there were a lot of adult bookstores along East Colfax Avenue in Denver. So, I got up enough courage and went inside one of them. I soon found out that if I paid the cashier inside one of these bookstores, he would let me slide and not worry if I was under eighteen! As time went on, just about all the cashiers at the different adult bookstores along East Colfax and Broadway knew who I was as a repeating customer and let me in to browse and buy. Like in the country-western song, "Looking for love in all the wrong places," I began looking for love and female acceptance in very wrong places. If I could not find it at school or anyplace else in the world, I would find it inside an adult bookstore.

> *My parents were not shy about talking to us kids about sex when we were growing up. But we also were told that it was a personal or family matter and not to talk about it to anyone else outside the family.*

The girls in the magazines would become my girlfriends. The women in the stag 8mm films were my girlfriends and lovers. The women in the sex novels were the women I was having sex fantasies with. But I never really understood what sexual intercourse was all about until I saw my first XXX adult movie. My parents told me about sexual intercourse and how it is done. But I couldn't grasp how the male privates functioned until I saw the X-rated movie and understood it. All the adult bookstores soon became my little heaven. While looking at the magazines or seeing an XXX hard-core film, there was no female rejection aimed toward me! I got accepted by those nude models and actresses up there on the screen. To me, there was no rejection and a lot of acceptance. But I didn't know that ALL the acceptance that I was feeling and experiencing was FALSE acceptance!

My addiction began in 1974 because I didn't know how to handle the rejection of girls. Plus, I had a low self-image of myself and bitter resentment toward the girls who pretended that they were interested in me but only wanted to make a fool out of me. My mindset concerning girls and dating was that I wasn't good enough or cool enough to be datable. To me, dating would be impossible because all females turned against me and wanted nothing to do with me. So, I closed my heart and chose to go fully into the world of sex and pornography. It became my own little private world. No female could hurt me. No female could put me down. No female could reject me. It was all open sex and love portrayed on the big screen. And I locked myself into a world of sexual pornographic fantasy. This was my world of escape from rejection and pain from girls. This went on all through my high school years, from a freshman to a senior. Even as a senior, on school breaks from the boarding academy, I'd take the train back to my aunt and uncle's house and visit all the porn places in Philadelphia to see the latest XXX movies.

When I was a senior in high school, I remember seeing one X-rated movie in Philadelphia from 1976–77, a movie that really turned me on. When I returned to school after the break, I smuggled these vile magazines back to my dorm. After I graduated high school and returned to

Denver, I fully dove back into pornography in bookstores and adult movie theaters. From 1978 to 1986, I saw many movies in adult movie theaters.

I started renting VHS porno videos and watching them in the 1980s and 1990s and collecting 8 mm stag films. Again, I was looking for love in all the wrong places. And fooling myself that I did find comfort in the world of magazines, sex novels, pictures, and sex films. Boy, what a wrong place to look for love!

CHAPTER 5

# The Power of Porn

If you remember the mid-1980s hit movie, *Back to the Future*, you will recall that in the first movie, there was a Top 40 pop song called "The Power of Love." This chapter will focus on "The Power of Pornography." Of how pornography has a power of its own to draw people into a belief and lifestyle that paints a false picture of what a true love relationship should be about.

The song is about the power of love, but pornography takes that power and turns it into raw lust. In pornography, you are not in love with a woman, you are lusting after a woman, thinking that sex is love. I had to learn the HARD WAY that sex is not love if you don't care for a woman and provide for her, being her best friend and always standing with her and behind her in all things. Pornography addicts think that sex is love. WRONG! I was wrong, wrong, wrong! Sex is the third step in a love relationship! If you really want a true, deep, love relationship with the girl of your dreams, then start with step one! Step one in a real love relationship is friendship. You must be her absolute best friend in whom she can fully trust. Work on friendship first, and then you are ready to move on to step two.

Step two is falling in love with that friend, period. Falling in love is not trying to please your sexual urges! Falling in love means that you care for her, constantly thinking about her, wanting to please her in a happy way, not a sexual way! Showing that you care by finding out what her favorite flowers are, what dress she likes, what music she enjoys listening to, and what her favorite dessert is—and then surprising her with them at an unexpected moment. This leads to step three: marriage is an expression of true love. Because sex in a legal marriage is an expression of true love!

Hardcore pornographers are totally backward on this whole approach. We want "sex only." Sex should always be an expression of true love. Lust is an expression of getting laid even if you don't really care for the girl, you just want to have a sexual experience to relieve your sexual desires. And pornography has tapped into that for lonely and rejected men! Keep reading, because I found out that pornography wasn't the answer that I thought it was to be in my life.

The pornography that I was exposed to played a major role in wanting to kidnap and rape Julie, though it wasn't the only influence. The very first time I was exposed to pornography was when I was about nine or ten years old. Every time I was at the home of my mother's friend, her only son Tony, who was three years older than I, invited my middle brother and me downstairs to the basement. That's where Tony set up his bedroom and showed us his newest monthly editions of *Playboy* magazines. At this point, however, I wasn't old enough to be turned on or get excited by looking at pictures of naked women, although I enjoyed looking at the beauty of the female form that God had made. But mostly, I was simply curious about what a woman's body looked like. *So, this is what a naked woman looks like,* I thought to myself.

Between the porn magazines, books, and movies, I was being exposed to rape fantasies, incest, bestiality, pedophilia, sex toys, women's scented body oils, X-rated jokes, and X-rated greeting cards. I was like a kid in a candy store. By the time I was eighteen, I had seen more than forty triple X-rated, full-length porn films and knew the "names" of all the porn stars.

My porn appetite grew stronger every year throughout the 1970s. But beginning in 1984, pornography left 70mm film to go to videotape. At that point, the movies lost any kind of storyline and plot and just featured straight sex on the screen. From that moment on, I lost most of my interest in seeing the new X-rated films and spent more time looking at 8mm stag films. But even they went to videotape in the early 1990s. After graduating high school, I worked at a couple of adult bookstores as a cashier and a film projectionist. Over the years, the bookstores became my hangouts. Other people use liquor, drugs, gambling, and food as escapes from their pain brought on by life, work, relationships, and poor self-image, all of which give them a skewed image of what life is all about. My escape was porn.

One thing I noticed in all my years of patronizing the adult bookstores was that everyone who came in had the same sad, lonely appearances as those who use drugs or alcohol. And they were all trying to find something to replace the same giant pain that I had. Customers involved in true hardcore porn all shared a common bond of broken relationships, misunderstandings of what true love is, low self-esteem, and a deep desire to be loved and accepted by the opposite sex. But over time, porn leads these people down paths they don't want to travel.

Customers usually started out with the soft-core, over-the-counter magazines like *Playboy* and *Penthouse*, then graduated to *Hustler* and *Oui*, which showed more explicit photos and contained more alluring sexual stories and cartoons. From there, they progressed to novels, gay pictures, sex toys, X-rated films, and adult videos. Typical hardcore customers were drawn into adult materials featuring homosexuality, bondage, and sex with a prostitute (male or female). Many of these folks sought to become prostitutes themselves, enter the adult movie business as actors, or—worst-case scenario—become a pedophile. This leads to the most dangerous level of porn, which features sex and the criminal mind: rape of both adults and children, including white slavery, kidnapping, date rape, and drug-induced rape.

Over the course of twenty-eight-plus years, porn nearly turned me into both a homosexual and a pedophile. I have seen about three hundred triple X-rated films and two hundred stag films or 8mm shorts. I've read approximately one hundred fifty porn novels and had unprotected sex with several prostitutes. Porn warped my mind so badly that I was deeply hooked on it, as one is deeply hooked on drugs and alcohol. It robbed me of my self-worth, of my ability to have a healthy relationship with any woman, and of my ability to respect women. I had no idea what a healthy sexual relationship was supposed to be. I've been engaged twice, but neither engagement progressed into marriage.

Pornography is a dead-end street. It promises you endless sexual pleasures that only lead to empty, bitter, standalone lives, complete with frustration and a sense of hopelessness—just like any drug that promises to take away pain and sorrow. It deceives the mind into thinking what it sees on the screen is true love and healthy sex. It convinces people that women want to be used as sex toys, sex objects, sex slaves, or only plain sex and discarded afterward. The woman is no longer a person with feelings of love or any type of emotion. Instead, she becomes a non-feeling human sex machine that exists only to give a man pleasure. Porn also knows that lesbian sex turns men on and leads men to believe all women like to have sex with other women. Eventually, porn debases the mind so far that men want to have sex with others of the same gender, animals, children, aliens, monsters, and basically, anything else suitably equipped. Porn is a power no one wants to play with!

CHAPTER 6

# The Beauty and the Beast

The song "I'm a Believer," written by Neil Diamond for the Monkees, describes all my relationships with women. I encourage you to read the lyrics online if you don't remember or know them.

I really believed love was only true in fairy tales and in some other person's life, just not mine. It always seemed love was out to get me, make a fool out of me. In every relationship I had with a woman, "disappointment haunted all of my dreams." Over the years of continual disappointment,

"I thought love was more or less a given thing." But it seemed the more I invested in a relationship, the less I got back. And that really hurt. After Carol, I reached a point of "What's the use in trying? All you get is pain!" My breakup with Carol caused more psychological damage than any of my other relationships. I spent four and a half months trying to get over the rejection from a girl I was ready to spend the rest of my life with.

And then I saw the face of Julie, a happy-go-lucky teenage girl. She had a certain charm and charisma that electrified me more than any woman ever had. Her very presence controlled me without her ever saying a word. I could never keep a secret from her, and I could never lie to her. That's how much influence and charm she had over me. I never felt that way around Carol, and I was engaged to her. But being around Julie just naturally made me want to tell her all of my hopes, dreams, and plans, all of my secrets, desires, wishes, and goals, as well as all of my faults, shortcomings, and failures. I wanted to tell her how much I'd fallen in love with her and how much I wanted to take care of her. I wanted to spend the rest of my life with her as her lover and her husband.

> *I really believed love was only true in fairy tales and in some other person's life, just not mine.*

In the story of the *Beauty and the Beast*, a man who is cursed to become an ugly monster falls in love with a beautiful young woman. But in order to have her, he must kidnap her and take her to his place of living, where he provides a beautiful room for her and tries to make her happy, hoping she'll fall in love with him. If she did, she would break the evil monster curse that was placed upon him. Julie was the "Beauty," and I was the "Beast." In my porn-deranged mind, I thought the only way I could get Julie's love was to kidnap and repeatedly rape her. After she'd sexually submitted to me, I'd take her back to my apartment and keep her there against her will until she fell in love and married me. Then I would take care of her for the rest of my life and provide for her as her husband and lover, just as the monster in the fairy tale would have taken care of the young maiden. But Julie only saw me as a monster, though I don't blame her after what I had done. She never knew how deeply I loved her or how much I wanted to take care of her and give her a man who would be loving and caring to her like Niles Crane was to Daphne Moon in the TV sitcom *Frasier*.

Someone reading this chapter might ask, "So, why didn't you just ask her out on a date, dummy?" Well, as you recall, in chapter two, I was forty-three, and she was eighteen. I didn't think I had a snowball's chance, and I couldn't handle that kind of rejection ... not again. So, in my mind, kidnapping her and impregnating her was the only way I could hopefully brainwash her into marrying me. Even though the beast had good intentions of providing her with a house, a car, furniture, nice clothes, jewelry, and anything else she wanted, none of it justified forcing her to give me the attention I wanted. I was the beast and acted like one!

In the 1980s, the Little River Band released a song called "Lonesome Loser." That's me! You can read the lyrics online. Every time I fall in love with an attractive gal, she becomes the queen of hearts, and I get dumped. I've been kicked down by girls all my life, but I keep getting back up again, still hoping there's at least one special woman out there who I could fall in love with and have as the love of my life. But generally, all women see me as a loser. I'm a good seventy to eighty pounds overweight; I don't have the perfect job with a fantastic money-making income; I don't live in a big, fancy house, and I don't own a Rolls Royce, a Jaguar, or a Porsche. In America's society, I'm a loser.

The last five sentences of "Lonesome Loser" describe my love life to a tee, and the cost was getting into pornography. I'd lived through rejection, putting on a happy face, even though the loneliness inside me was driving me crazy. I don't know that I'll ever have a woman I can open up to like I wanted to with Julie. In my twenty-eight years of hard pornography and unprotected sex with female prostitutes, I didn't want to show any woman the sick porn I was into, but anyone who watched me closely back then could see it all. I'd hoped that someday someone, like the love of my life, or even God, would see me for me. I took a hard look at myself when I was in prison.

While in prison, I had the chance to really get reacquainted with God again. That was the change in my life. Making God first in your life changes everything! Being somebody or becoming somebody means a change of lifestyle and commitment, which I'll go into in chapters eight through twelve. Someone did look inside of me, saw everything, and forgave me. That was God! I'm not running and hiding from my crime or my involvement in pornography. Quite the contrary, I'm hoping anyone who is currently involved in pornography will read this book, see the light, and find the way out before they commit a crime and end up in prison as I did.

CHAPTER 7

# Why Men Like to Watch Sex

This chapter is the hardest one to write out of all the chapters in this book. And the last chapter on my sex life. I came across a book that came out in print in 2002, the year I got locked up. The book by David Loftus is called "Watching Sex—How Men Really Respond to Pornography." Using Loftus's book and my own past experiences, both of us will try to explain why men like to watch sex. There are a lot of different reasons why men watch pornography. And you cannot pinpoint it to one just reason: that men are just plain lustful! I told you the reason why I turned to pornography was I felt that the whole female race was against me, didn't like me, and rejected me. For men, there are different reasons than in my case. Some like to watch, some are curious, some think it's artful or artistic. Some men don't like it. Some men like me get educated on it. But what drives men to look and watch pornography is more than just hot babes up on the screen or posing in a picture shot.

One factor could be how they were raised and if their parents openly talked about sex in front of their children. Or did they learn about it in school or off the streets, hanging around a group of rough, tough kids? Or were they so protected and sheltered by it from their parents that they couldn't know anything about sex until their wedding night? In David's book, he explores many aspects of why men respond to pornography. The aspects are: how they were raised, content of sexuality, how it happened, and initial reactions. Parents' attitudes, social messages about porn, men's taste, and what they want to see more of. Why "lesbian" seems are so popular, and reactions to men in these scenes. The issue of the penis size, how men use pornography, how often, correlation to mood, masturbation, and feelings after use. Sharing porn, use and discussion with other men, attitudes of use by, and discussion with significant others. Men who like special kinds of pornography. Question of addiction, periods of lesser or greater use, reality versus fantasy. Pornography as hell or pornography as therapy. All these are aspects of why men like to watch or see a nude woman or a man having sexual intercourse with a woman.

Now we will get into "fantasy rape" or "forced sex against a woman's will." This plays into this stupid idea that a man has to be dominant in sex with any woman. That the woman is always weak and submissive and must be ruled and controlled. It also gives the false idea that women like to be raped. But again, we must remove the false acting of those on the screen or in a picture magazine from reality. These are paid actors, faking it just to arouse you sexually. But the tide is turning that more men like to see and watch lesbian rape where a lesbian rapes a straight, non-lesbian woman against her will.

And then there is bondage rape. A lot of men like to watch a woman tied up and raped by a man, or a woman tied up and raped by a lesbian woman. But why do you ask? Here's why! Because it gives the very false idea that if you force yourself on a woman, the unwilling party will break down during the forced act.

These are targeted at society rejects and Fifth Avenue losers. Men who are not attractive, who have a fat belly, short men, men that are not athletic, or in the high society crowd. The non "James Dean" men that women don't like or find unattractive physically. So, what is the solution to this problem? In pornography, it's fantasy rape or forced sex because a woman like that has to submit. But again, it's dominance and dominance paramount. Being in control of a woman and having her being totally submissive gives the male power. And many men like having that power.

But mostly, men like to watch sex because it's geared toward men who are society rejects or homosexual men. In my twenty-eight years of being involved in pornography, I did see a few single females viewing it. But it is mostly men who are involved.

Pornography is a lie! Pornography says, "Pay me first, then I'll give you all the sex you want!"

The same is true with a prostitute—pay me, and I'll have sex with you. Why do men like to watch pornography? It is because they are fascinated with it. To some, it's an art, to others, it's exciting, but to a lot of men is because they've been hurt, lonely, or society rejects, and they are looking for love and acceptance. Which brings us to our next chapter.

CHAPTER 8

# An Introduction to God

The title of this chapter alone will turn off a lot of men. Why are you bringing religion into this? What does God have to do with pornography? Are you going to tell us that God hates pornographers and pedophiles, and perverted people who like sex all the time? Are you going to tell us that we are going to burn in hell forever if we don't do what God says?

Most men have an incorrect view of God. They don't know who He is or what He's about. God never invented "religion." Man did. So why bring God into this? Because He's the only one who can help you overcome pornography and its deadly side effects, and He does so without judging you. God found me at the Harris County Jail when I wasn't looking for Him. One day I had a mental and emotional breakdown resulting from fear. I didn't know what the future held for me. But God spoke to me, and I heard His voice say, "You are My son," three times in a row. And then He said, "I have a reason why you must go through this but be brave, and in the end, I will use you." Only my late father has ever called me "son," so I knew it was God's voice reassuring me that all was not lost, that I was forgiven, and that He loved me. That was the day I started reading the Bible.

God's enemy hates God so much that he wants you to hate Him too. He wants you to have nothing to do with Him. But those who have been hurt, lonely, and rejected by society are just the kind of people God's looking for. He wants only one thing of you—to become your friend—but not just your friend: to be your best friend in the whole world. He wants you to trust Him with all of your secrets, hopes, desires, dreams, plans, wishes, and goals. He wants you to trust Him so much that you will run to Him for advice on any subject. God is a God of love, even though His enemy says He's a God of hate, ready to strike down anyone who doesn't follow His rules! Don't be fooled by the enemy's lies. God's love is indescribable and unconditional!

> *But those who have been hurt, lonely, and rejected by society are just the kind of people God's looking for.*

The Greek word for godly love is "Agape" (A-ga-pay). God loved humanity so much that He paid the ultimate sacrifice, and now He's seeking an ultimate friendship with you. Yeah, but isn't worship a religion? NO! People worship cars, money, rock groups, and sports, but they don't make a religion out of it!

There is only one true God, not thousands of different gods as Satan has introduced around the world. God has a government built on the principle of agape love. The problem is, we as human beings can use the single word "love" in more than fourteen different ways! That becomes very confusing when trying to pin down a specific meaning in describing it. The old Greek word of agape (love), however, is a "selfless specific," "unconditional love," and "love for others without any rewards attached to it" with no sexual feelings involved in it.

Real love is always absent in the heart of mankind unless placed there by God through the reception of the Holy Spirit. "And hope maketh not ashamed; because the love of God is shed abroad in our hearts by the Holy Ghost which is given unto us" (Rom. 5:5). It is a love of divine origin and will always seek to serve and never to be served or to be noticed. It's patient without cause, always forgiving no matter who's at fault, and always ready to lend a hand. It always has your best interest at heart and will always look after and protect you if you allow God to be your friend. He will never leave you, never point an accusing finger at you, never put you down, and never turn His back on you.

To be His true best friend, you'll have to give everything over to Him, and people don't want to do that. They believe the lie that says, "I don't need God in my life." Or, "I'll be His friend, but I won't surrender everything to Him!" But God wants a close relationship with you. He loves you and wants your total love in return. He wants you to be His and no one else's, just like a spouse. But because of His great agape love for us, God gives us the choice to enter into that love relationship or not. In the meantime, He patiently waits and woos us to His love. He actually sheds that love abroad in our hearts and promises that if we submit to Him, we can resist the devil, and he will flee from us! "Submit yourselves therefore to God. Resist the devil, and he will flee from you" (James 4:7).

But why should I accept Him or even love Him? What has He done for me personally that I should appreciate Him as God? The answer to that question is found in the next chapter.

CHAPTER 9

# Understanding the Bible

The Bible is God's Word to us. Its purpose is to communicate who God is, His love and will for our lives, and what sin has done to humanity. From Genesis to Revelation, God has shown us what sin does to those who choose to follow their wayward wills, those who fail to understand that the heart is deceitful, and "There is a way which seemeth right unto a man, but the end thereof are the ways of death" (Prov. 14:12). Remember, God is a God of pure love who never wants to hurt anyone, even though His enemy tries to tell you that He is an evil, hardheaded, extracting dictator! One slip-up, and wham! God strikes you down!

So, what is sin? Any wrong act to please self while hurting others or yourself at the same time. We all seek pleasure in the wrong things. Webster's definition is: "an offense against religious or moral law" or "transgression of the law of God." Scripture declares that "sin is the transgression of the law" (1 John 3:4) and that "All unrighteousness is sin" (1 John 5:17). It is also clear that "Therefore to him that knoweth to do good, and doeth it not, to him it is sin" (James 4:17) and "The wages of sin is death" (Rom. 6:23). The Bible clearly reveals what sin does to us. "Behold, the Lord's hand is not shortened, that it cannot save; neither his ear heavy, that it cannot hear: But your iniquities have separated between you and your God, and your sins have hid his face from you, that he will not hear" (Isa. 59:1–2). And "If I regard iniquity in my heart, the Lord will not hear me" (Ps. 66:18), etc. This brings us to a very vital question: how did sin originate, and who is responsible for sin?

God's enemy is called "Satan," or the accuser. Unfortunately, sin started in heaven with an angel named Lucifer, who was jealous of God's position in heaven and wanted to be higher than He was and wanted to take over and control everything. He wanted to be God. "For you have said in your heart: 'I will ascend into heaven, I will exalt my throne above the stars of God; I will also sit on the mount of the congregation On the farthest sides of the north; I will ascend above the heights of the clouds, I will be like the Most High'" (Isa. 14:13–14 NKJV). The Bible declares that "War broke out in heaven: Michael and his angels fought with the dragon; and the dragon and his angels fought, … So the great dragon was cast out, that serpent of old, called the Devil and Satan, who deceives the whole world" (Rev. 12:7, 9 NKJV). We further discover that Satan was:

> [T]he anointed cherub that covereth; and I have set thee so: thou wast upon the holy mountain of God; thou hast walked up and down in the midst of the stones of fire. Thou wast perfect in thy ways from the day that thou wast created, till iniquity was found in thee. By the multitude of thy merchandise they have filled the midst of thee with violence, and thou hast sinned: therefore

> I will cast thee as profane out of the mountain of God: and I will destroy thee, O covering cherub, from the midst of the stones of fire. Thine heart was lifted up because of thy beauty, thou hast corrupted thy wisdom by reason of thy brightness: I will cast thee to the ground, I will lay thee before kings, that they may behold thee. Thou hast defiled thy sanctuaries by the multitude of thine iniquities, by the iniquity of thy traffick; therefore will I bring forth a fire from the midst of thee, it shall devour thee, and I will bring thee to ashes upon the earth in the sight of all them that behold thee. All they that know thee among the people shall be astonished at thee: thou shalt be a terror, and never shalt thou be any more. (Ezek. 28:14–19)

God cast him out of heaven, and he's been called Satan, or the devil, ever since. When God created the first pair of human beings, Adam and Eve, Satan wanted them to disobey God's warning to them. Why do parents give warnings to little children? For their protection from any danger that would inflict pain upon them. For example, you tell your four-year-old son not to touch the red-hot electric burner because you know he likes red and likes to touch things that are bright red. But if little Tommy disobeys Mommy's or Daddy's warning and touches it, what happens? You know the answer.

But eating the fruit of the forbidden tree was not only a warning but a test to see whether Adam and Eve really loved God, who created them, and whether they would obey His command out of that love for Him. He gave Adam and Eve the full right to freely choose to love Him or not. Not to serve Him out of force or fear, but because they loved Him. Eve knew the consequences of eating that fruit! Genesis records how Eve was tempted by the devil (the serpent): "And when the woman saw that the tree was good for food, and that it was pleasant to the eyes" (Gen. 3:6).

When we are tempted to commit a sin, we think of only one person, and that's ourselves, and we shut out everyone else. We could care less who we are hurting because I'm enjoying this moment of self-gratification.

Because of Satan, Eve believed God lied to her and Adam about the penalty for eating the fruit and felt God was holding something wonderful back from them. She also reasoned that if God were really a God of love, He would not hold this thing back from them.

After Eve had eaten the fruit, she tempted Adam with it, and he ate it, too. That's how sin entered our world—by Adam and Eve's wrongful acts of seeking pleasure instead of heeding God's warning not to eat of that tree. Sin has separated humanity from God's true love ever since. From Genesis to Revelation, God shows how sinful people's actions really are. The stories of Cain and Abel, the worldwide flood, the tower of Babel, Sodom and Gomorrah, Balaam, the kings of Israel and Judah, Queen Jezebel, as well as Esther and Daniel all show what sin does to us and how badly we hurt other people for personal pleasure or gain.

We are the children of Adam and Eve because they are the parents of the whole human race, and every child born from them from the time of the Garden of Eden until now is born into sin. We, as children of our parents, are sinners by inheritance. We can choose to sin; it's in our nature to do it. We have the option of whether to sin or not to sin! There is an escape from sin if you want it. It's our nature to sin because of our fallen nature. But the devil doesn't want you to understand that you can overcome sin. He does not want you to understand that when we sin, it's because we have chosen to. Even our culture doesn't recognize every human has a sin problem. The devil is deceiving the whole world by making everyone think we have a good nature and just do a few bad things here and there. And the whole world believes this lie! The Bible clearly shows that by nature, we are not good people and that all of us have a sickness, called sin, passed to us by Adam and Eve.

But God didn't throw up His arms after Adam and Eve sinned and say, "Oh well, both Adam and Eve disobeyed me; there's nothing that I can do about it. I guess they're going to get what they deserve. There is no hope for them now!" He had an "emergency backup plan" that even the devil didn't know about. It was called "The Plan of Salvation" or

"Redemption of Mankind," which God immediately put into effect to save both Adam and Eve and the entire human race from sin.

The Bible is divided into the Old and New Testaments; the book of Genesis in the Old Testament tells of the plan of salvation and of the coming of a redeemer who would deliver the entire human race out of the hand of Satan and sin and back into the hand of God. That redemption is what the New Testament is all about. So, who is this Savior God points to in the Old Testament? His name is Jesus Christ, God's own Son. What Christ did affected the entire human race, from Adam and Eve up to the present and onward. He freed human beings from the power of sin and wrongdoing. See how in the next chapter.

> *What Christ did affected the entire human race, from Adam and Eve up to the present and onward.*

CHAPTER 10

# God's Son Can Help You!

The Bible reveals what it calls the Godhead, or what many refer to today as the Trinity, consisting of the Father, Son, and Holy Spirit! God the Father, God the Son, and God the Holy Spirit act in love for fallen humanity even though each plays a different role. As we talked about in the last chapter, God set forth the plan of salvation to save mankind from sin and its penalty—death!

Adam and Eve both knew the penalty and understood what death meant—physical, non-existing death, not just spiritual death as some pastors or Bible teachers teach. A physical, non-existing, second death is the penalty for sin. But knowing this, Adam and Eve still sinned, thinking God lied to them about death. You see, there is a spiritual world that is much, much different than our physical world. We see and know the physical world, but the spiritual world is invisible to our human eyes. Now, in reading God's Word, or the Bible, to mankind, we see that Jesus stepped in when Adam sinned and assumed Adam's penalty be placed on Him! It was as if a man was sentenced to die, and a total stranger stepped in out of the blue and said, "Let him go and live, and I will die in his place." Or, "I will take the penalty and die in his place. He doesn't have to die. I will die in his place, and he can go on living." That is why Adam and Eve didn't suddenly fall over dead, like they should have, after eating the forbidden fruit. God, or Jesus, looked down on the earth from heaven and saw Adam and Eve eating the forbidden fruit and immediately stepped in and took the penalty that should have been theirs. If He hadn't, Adam and Eve would have immediately died. Out of love God gave them a second chance.

The New Testament teaches that Jesus became the "second Adam" for humanity. The first Adam brought sin and woe to every human being. From the fall on, humans had no choice; they were stuck with the results of sin! However, Jesus Christ, the second Adam, has taken away the sin problem and its penalty for every human being who believes that Christ died for them personally. Everyone can be set free from sin and its power even though not everyone believes it. This is a free gift from God to all mankind that is handed to every human being from the foundations of the world. We just have to believe it is so. We are born forgiven from Adam's penalty!

That does not mean, however, that everyone will go to heaven. The Universalists teach the theory that if everyone is saved, then everyone will be in heaven, but they're only half right. While everyone is saved from Adam's penalty of eternal death, Jesus himself said in the New Testament that not everyone is going to be saved and live in heaven because God has given all human beings the choice to believe in the gift that God has already given us or to reject it. Please remember that our love relationship with God exists because He loved us first. People will be lost because of not believing in Jesus Christ as a personal Savior and refusing to accept the free gift He gave them before they ever asked.

Two thousand years ago, Jesus was born here on earth as both God and man in one human body of flesh and blood like ours. He lived and died, taking the penalty that the human race should have received—death—eternal separation from God! In addition, Jesus, who knows firsthand what we are going through, knows what temptation is, "For we do not have a High Priest [Jesus Christ] who cannot sympathize with our weaknesses, but was in all points tempted as we are, yet without sin" (Heb. 4:15 NKJV). The devil threw every temptation at Him you can think of: sexual temptations, rejection temptations, self-power temptations, get-even temptations, and all other temptations, but Jesus endured them all and never fell into sin. Now, Jesus is here to help us overcome any temptation that comes our way. He wants us to totally rely on Him. "Casting all your care upon him; for he careth for you" (1 Peter 5:7).

Jesus not only wants us to choose to love and serve Him as our God but wants us to truly believe that He alone can help us in every aspect of our lives. Not only does He want our love, but He also wants to be our best and closest friend that we share everything with and trust completely. "Come unto me, all ye that labour and are heavy laden, and I will give you rest" (Matt. 11:28). Remember, it takes more than just believing that God or Jesus Christ is real or that He exists. Singular is clear: "Thou believest that there is one God; thou doest well: the devils also believe, and tremble" (James 2:19).

A lot of people feel their belief is good enough, but belief without any action is useless; it is dead. "What good is it, my brothers and sisters, if someone claims to have faith but has no deeds? Can such faith save them?" "In the same way, faith by itself, if it is not accompanied by action, is dead. But someone will say, 'You have faith; I have deeds.' Show me your faith without deeds, and I will show you my faith by my deeds" (James 2:14, 17–18 NIV). Jesus is freely offering you help, but you must act on that belief to get the help. You can believe all you want that a blender works, but if it is not plugged into the wall, will it still work? Jesus wants our faith in Him to be plugged into the "spiritual socket" to receive His power to help us out of our temptations and any other problems in our lives.

CHAPTER 11

# Asking for Forgiveness

In this next to the last chapter of the book, I'll be asking, "Which is more important: Getting God's forgiveness or getting my victim's forgiveness?" As for me personally, I would like to have BOTH! As you see, when I went back to court back at the end of 2008 and into 2009, the city of Houston spent ninety days searching for Julie and her parents to contact them, letting them know to come to court and argue against "the defense." That's me. They, the city of Houston, couldn't find them at all! It seemed that they "raptured" from the face of the earth! Since she had disappeared, the case of "Kidnapping with Sexual Intent" charge was dismissed.

But getting back to forgiveness, God wants us humans to forgive one another! God forgives, but why does He forgive? The answer is "God is Love." God is a loving God, and He does not want us to be lost! He died for us that we might live forever with Him! Remember what John 3:16 says, "For God so loved the world, that he gave his only begotten Son, that whosoever believeth in him should not perish, but have everlasting life." God was in Christ reconciling the world to Himself, "All things are of God, who hath **reconciled us** to himself by Jesus Christ, and hath given to us the ministry of reconciliation" (2 Cor. 5:18). "The Lord is not slack concerning his promise, as some men count slackness; but is longsuffering to usward, not willing that any should perish, but that all should come to repentance" (2 Peter 3:9). Also, "My little children, these things write I unto you, that ye sin not. And if any man sin, we have an advocate with the Father, Jesus Christ the righteous" (1 John 2:1). In Greek there are four (4) different words for love: eros, philia, storge, and agape.

Agape is a love that comes from God and centers on God! It's a godly love without any self attached to it!

> *Agape is a love that comes from God and centers on God!*

But you say, "I'm a murder; can God forgive me?" Or you say, "I'm a rapist; can God forgive me?" Or "I am a thief; can God forgive me?" There is nothing you have ever done or can ever do that will cause God to cease loving you! Nothing He will not forgive! Listen to this, "In him [Christ] we have redemption through his blood, **the forgiveness of our trespasses**, [or wrongdoing] according to the riches of his grace" (Eph. 1:7 ESV), or "in whom we have redemption, **the forgiveness of sins**" (Col.1:14 ESV), or "who desires all people to be **saved** and to **come to the knowledge of the truth**" (1 Tim. 2:4 ESV), or "The saying is trustworthy and deserving of full acceptance, that Christ Jesus came into the world to save **sinners**, of whom **I am the foremost**" (1 Tim. 1:15 ESV, all emphases mine). Jesus Christ and God the Father can forgive, but sometimes it's hard for humans to forgive! I don't know if Julie will ever forgive me. I've scarred her for life.

What I want to tell my reading audience is that Julie had a very strong influence upon me that was not just a mere crush or infatuation. I really fell head over heels in love with her. I wished that I could marry her and tell her every day that I'm sorry for what I did to her and ask for her forgiveness. Every time I hear the song by Phil Collins, "Take a Look at Me," I immediately think of Julie because of the lyrics of that song. They embrace my feelings that she will never know. Look up the song online and read the lyrics.

Touching on forgiveness, I want to leave you some more Bible texts on what God says about forgiveness. "But with you there is **forgiveness**, that you may be feared" (Ps. 130:4 ESV, emphasis mine).

"To the Lord our God belong mercy and **forgiveness**, for we have rebelled against him" (Dan. 9:9 ESV).

"For this is my blood of the covenant, which is poured out for many for the **forgiveness** of sins" (Matt. 26:28 ESV).

"John appeared, baptizing in the wilderness and proclaiming a baptism of repentance for the **forgiveness** of sins" (Mark 1:4 ESV).

"To give knowledge of salvation to his people in the **forgiveness** of their sins" (Luke 1:77 ESV).

"And Peter said to them, 'Repent and be baptized every one of you in the name of Jesus Christ for the **forgiveness** of your sins, and you will receive the gift of the Holy Spirit.'" (Acts 2:38 ESV).

"To him all the prophets bear witness that everyone who believes in him receives **forgiveness** of sins through his name" (Acts 10:43 ESV).

"Let it be known to you therefore, brothers, that through this man **forgiveness** of sins is proclaimed to you" (Acts 13:38 ESV). There is only one sin God will not forgive, only one unpardonable sin. That is the unconfessed sin! Will you confess all of them to Him today?

CHAPTER 12

# God or the Twelve-Step Program?

A lot of our readers will ask what is the most effective way to overcome or quit porno? A lot of people would say the "Twelve-Step Program." I have a friend back in Houston who was a sex offender, and he is working for SAA (Sex Addicts Anonymous). He went through the Twelve-Step Program and swears by it! But I got over it by only turning to God! So, do you need both the Twelve-Step and God? And again, a lot of people would say yes! Let's look at the Twelve-Step Program. They do recognize that there is a God, but not a personal God! Their main focal point is on you changing under your own willpower to do it! They call it steps, but you are forcing yourself to change under your own power alone! NO HELP FROM GOD, it's you alone, and YOU CAN ACHIEVE IT! attitude.

It's like patting yourself on the back, saying that I've achieved in overcoming porno! Self and forcing yourself to change is their motto instead of a total surrender to God to change me, and that's what God is looking for—allowing Him (God) to change you and not yourself changing you. Remember what Philippians 4:13 says, "I can do all things through Christ who strengthens me" (NKJV). Not "God will help those who help themselves or make it a priority to change themselves under their own willpower"! What people in this world do not want to talk about is the root problem that we have that deals with crime, pornography, murder, theft, robbery, and evil is all due to SIN. And nobody in this world wants to talk about sin! How did SIN start? Can we blame God for that?

Human philosophers for years like Plato, Socrates, Aristotle, and others tried to explain what evil is apart from God. Is God evil? No! We find in the Bible that God is "Love." But God does have an enemy called Satan or the devil! Did God create Satan or the devil? No! The word "Satan" in Latin is diabolical or mostly devil. The word "devil" is deceiver. We find out in the Bible that all of creation, the stars, planets, worlds, universes, atoms, everything was through God's only son, Jesus Christ. But before that, God and His Son created angels that are up in heaven. One angel was called Lucifer, meaning light bearer! He was the most loved and the highest angel out of all the other angels up in heaven!

We also find out that if God, through His Son, created intelligent life, as in humans or angels or other intelligent life on other planets that we don't know about, God gave each one the power of choice! To love someone, we must choose that, and in God's government of love, the intelligent beings must have the right of choice! God is not forcing His love on any intelligent beings. But the right to choose to accept it or not is always there. We find out in the book of Isaiah that Lucifer had a "self" problem.

He looked at himself and started to admire himself and his abilities to the point that he wanted to overthrow God's government and be like God Himself and to rule others! We read in Isaiah 14:12–15, "How you are fallen from heaven, O Lucifer, son of the morning! How you are cut down to the ground, You who weakened the nations! For you have said in your heart: 'I will ascend into heaven, I will exalt my throne above the stars of God; I will also sit on the mount of the congregation On the farthest sides of the north; I will ascend above the heights of the clouds, I will be like the Most High.' Yet you shall be brought down to Sheol, (grave) To the lowest depths of the Pit" (NKJV).

Count how many "I"s that are there. There are five of them! Lucifer had an "I" problem! Self was getting in the way of his thinking and judgment. When Adam and Eve were created here on earth, they were filled with "agape" (selfless) love! As a mystery to God, Lucifer was the one who started sin up in heaven by rebelling against God and His government of love, which is agape or total selflessness! There is no self in agape! But when Satan lied or tricked Eve into eating the forbidden fruit, that's when agape went out the back door and self came in to replace it!

Self cannot serve God at all! Self hates God, period. Self wants nothing to do with God. Self is with Satan in hating God. When Adam and Eve ate the fruit and turned the world over to Satan, that's when evil started here on earth! SIN is living apart from God and wanting nothing to do with Him. The true definition of what SIN is, according to the Bible, is breaking His holy Law, which is the ten commandments. 1 John 3:4 says, "Whosoever committeth sin transgresseth also the law: for sin is the transgression of the law." Earth is the only planet out of all the other planets in the whole universe or galaxy that has a SIN problem! But again, we find in the Bible that God had a backup plan if human beings ever fell to sin. Jesus would come to this earth as a human being and die the death penalty that was placed on us human beings from the start. Thus, forever freeing us from the power of sin that's in us!

But for that to happen, we have to fully surrender ourselves to God daily for Him to control us through His Holy Spirit. We have to "die" daily or die to self daily. God can control us by us allowing Him to come in and run our lives, not self! But in the Twelve-Step, very little is on God, but mostly on self, and making self-choices to improve yourself is their main priority! Right now, go to God in prayer and admit that you are a sinner, and you need to be forgiven, and accept Jesus Christ as your personal Savior for what He has done for you!

# Why I Wrote This Kind of a Book?

The reason I wrote this book is NOT to claim that I got away with committing a sexual crime and how I did it. NO, no, no, no! This book is for sexual perverts like me who have serious pornography problems. You just read my short biography of how I was addicted to porno for twenty-eight years. Not soft pornography, but hard pornography! I fell into it after rejection by and love for the women. This led me to do what I tried to do to my victim. This book is for men or women who have a pornography problem and cannot quit!

*Pornography is NOT THE ANSWER!*

Don't end up like I did, trying to rape someone out of love and deep affection! It's not worth it. You will ruin your life and deeply regret what you did for the rest of your life! Pornography is NOT THE ANSWER!

Pornography is a total flat-out LIE! It cons both lonely and sexually addicted people! Pornography is a multi-billion-dollar-a-year business industry because they know that there are suckers out there who will buy it and believe in it! It's very misleading and will deceive you into believing that normal human beings act that way! But there is help for those who have a deep pornography problem, those who are hard-core addicts as I was to overcome it. There is power through JESUS CHRIST, the Son of God, who died for you so that you can be forgiven and start a new life over again as I did.

Don't believe that you don't need God or any type of religion, that you can walk away from it under your own power. No, you must admit that you have an addiction to pornography and that you need God's help through His Son Jesus Christ. You don't know how much God, through His Son Jesus, wants to heal you from your pornography addiction once and for all ever! You can be totally free from pornography. But God is never going to force you to come to Him or give up pornography. The choice is yours to make!!

There is a God who created this earth in six literal days, and all of us, unfortunately, inherit the sin from our first parents, Adam and Eve. God's great love for us caused Him to send His only begotten Son to redeem us from our sins so we can start afresh, leaving the old things behind and overcoming the things that we thought were impossible because of the power it had over us! You must make a solid choice for God to help you! And then believe that He will help you! "I can do all things through Christ who strengthens me" (Phil. 4:13 NKJV). "You are of God, little children, and have overcome them, because He who is in you is greater than he who is in the world" (1 John 4:4 NKJV). "Jesus came and spake unto them, saying, 'All power is given unto me in heaven and in earth'" (Matt. 28:18). "And whatever you ask in My name, that I will do, that the Father may be glorified in the Son. If you ask anything in My name, I will do it" (John 14:13–14 NKJV).

Remember that 2,000 years ago that Christ died on the cross for YOUR SINS, not His! Go to Him in prayer and offer up this prayer to Him now.

PRAYER

Oh, Father in heaven,
I have a terrible pornography problem
I like to watch pornography on the Internet, watch
Pornography in the adult bookstores, read porno

novel books. I need Your help; I need Your Son's help!
Jesus died for my sins on the cross, and I believe that He
died just for me. Make me an overcomer over porno, and
give me victory over it! Thank You for hearing my prayer.
All of this I ask will be done in the name of Your Son, Jesus Christ.
Amen.

If you pray this prayer, God will honor it and will give you the grace and power to stop this addiction that you have. I praise God that through Jesus Christ's power alone, I have overcome my terrible pornography addiction. And now I want to share it with others. That is the reason I wrote this book.

# A Day

It was maybe the third or fourth week since I had been arrested and inside the first jail pod at the Harris County Jail Facility. And I remember that one day, I don't know which day of the week it was, but one day I was so scared and depressed from not knowing what was going to happen in the future that I was losing it mentally! Crying and weeping, lying on the mattress on the floor, my world was coming apart, and I could do nothing about it. Then suddenly, I heard a great loud voice with a deep, authoritative bass voice inside of my head that said,

"You are my son!"

"You are my son!"

"You are my son! And I have you in here for a reason! If you can survive your prison time, you will know why."

The voice kind of shocked me at first, and I thought that my mind was playing tricks on me! I knew that my real father passed away when I was twelve years old. But the more I pondered it, I got a peace of mind and hope back again! I realized that it was God or His Holy Spirit speaking to me! God didn't give up on me for what I had done! He wanted me and reminded me again that I was His son through the death of His own Son, Jesus Christ! That experience alone made me want to read and learn more of what the Bible says. With that knowledge I could face what was coming to me and live with it.

# Appendix

## Tuesday March 19, 2002, *Houston Chronicle* Newspaper Metropolitan (Area briefs) Section

### Area briefs

**Taxi driver is charged in kidnapping, assault**

An independent taxi driver has been charged with aggravated kidnapping and aggravated assault in an alleged attack on a passenger.

Dale Edward Stivers, 43, of the 300 block of Parramatta Lane was arrested Friday and held in lieu of $30,000 bail.

Harris County sheriff's detectives said an 18-year-old woman reported Feb. 23 she was abducted and assaulted while a passenger in Stivers' cab.

**2 killed when car flips several times, hits tree**

Two people were killed when their car veered off a northeast Houston road while trying to pass, flipped several times and hit a tree.

They were Artemio Caballero, 23, of the 9700 block of Debbie Lane and Cherie Nicole Peterson, 14, of the 1400 block of Nashua.

The accident occurred just after midnight Sunday in the 2100 block of West Little York.

**Wreck kills teen-ager on her way to school**

A high school sophomore on her way to classes was killed a few blocks from her northeast Harris County home when she failed to yield at a stop sign, deputy sheriffs said.

Julie Gilstrap, 16, of the 7200 block of Glen Falls died in the 7500

tal shooting of a man outside his southwest Houston apartment.

Argimiro Baeza, 40, of the 6400 block of West Bellfort was drinking beer with friends in the parking lot about 7 p.m. Sunday when Baeza was shot in the chest, police said.

**3 suspects are sought in slaying of shopper**

Houston police are searching for three men who fatally assaulted a shopper.

Jose Antonio Galvan, 28, and his wife were shopping in the 13000 block of the Northwest Freeway about 11 p.m. Saturday when they began arguing with female shoppers. One threatened to have her husband physically assault Galvan, who left with his wife.

Later, three men approached Galvan and one punched him in the head while the other two kicked him, witnesses said. Galvan fell and suffered a head injury. He died in Memorial Hermann Hospital.

**Channelview man dies, passenger hurt in crash**

A Channelview man was killed and another man was injured when their car struck a metal culvert, went airborne and slammed into a utility pole.

Alejandro Martinez, of the 1800 block of Amy Michelle, was the passenger in the car that left the 16000 block of Wallisville at 11:20 p.m. Saturday.

Martinez died and the driver, Baltazar Gutierrez, was injured, police said.

**Head-on collision kills**

www.TEACHServices.com • (800) 367-1844

We invite you to view the complete
selection of titles we publish at:
**www.TEACHServices.com**

We encourage you to write us
with your thoughts about this,
or any other book we publish at:
**info@TEACHServices.com**

TEACH Services' titles may be purchased in
bulk quantities for educational, fund-raising,
business, or promotional use.
**bulksales@TEACHServices.com**

Finally, if you are interested in seeing
your own book in print, please contact us at:
**publishing@TEACHServices.com**

We are happy to review your manuscript at no charge.